Praise for Reverse Head

"A great read for any senior executive looking to move their career forward. Full of practical advice with real insights into what steps to take to maximise personal marketability and deal with recruiters and head hunters effectively."

Phil Sharp, Executive Head Hunter

"I read once that the skill of learning subtraction and division is that you are 'reversing' the natural order of additions. The same applies to 'reverse headhunting'. If you think that common sense about headhunting cannot be written down and that you have read it all, then read this book and think again. If you think that common sense about headhunting can be learnt, then read this book and benefit from it. This book will help you develop a better way to 'headhunt' your way to your next role."

Isaac Alfon, Senior Risk Manager

"This book is a very useful and valuable tool. It explains and lists the different ways and parameters which the applicant for a new position will have to deal with. It gives very good advice, a high level view as well as practical tips, and avoids the candidate making mistakes and losing opportunities."

Alain Ferrandi, CFO

"Reverse Headhunting is a very practical reference, particularly useful for the executives who have not had a need to deal with recruiters or faced a job interview for a long time. The book helps you to prepare for interview situations and to answer questions you did not have to consider previously.

References to other material expand this work making it a broad forum of information. I wish to acknowledge also that I personally am a beneficiary of Steven's assistance in my career transition."

Les Michalik, CEO

"As a senior manager involved in recruitment and head count re-organisations as part of my Sales Management role, when it came to planning my next move as the result of a redundancy I felt very ill equipped to find my next position. The logical approach used by Steve Nicholls and outlined in this book gave me selection of ideas I could build on and use to plan my next move and proactively manage my career. This is a great book, easy to read and full of useful ideas that inspire action."

Steve Bastow, Commercial Manager

"At last; sound and wide-ranging advice for the senior job-seeker in one well-written package! A fantastic tool-kit and a 'must read' book for any senior executive who is looking, or forced to look, for their next role. Steve's social media strategy chapter, especially the 'how to' tactics in regard to leveraging LinkedIn, is well thought through and pragmatic advice. Building and using your network for referrals is emphasized and explained in plain language: job-seekers should take note and do it! Equally good is the exhortation to "build your brand" and the importance of this element in 'selling yourself' to decision-makers. All-in-all, a great read and deserves a space on the senior job-seekers book shelf."

Rob Young, Staffing Solutions Provider

REVERSE
HEADHUNTING

STEVE NICHOLLS

V1.0

ISBN 9781500729929
Executive Careers Publishing.

Contents

Thanks   6

Foreword   7

Introduction   9

CHAPTER 1 - Career Coaching   15

CHAPTER 2 - Personal Branding   23

CHAPTER 3 - CV/Resume   41

CHAPTER 4 - The Hidden Jobs Market   53

CHAPTER 5 - LinkedIn & other Social Media   59

CHAPTER 6 - Jobs boards   75

CHAPTER 7 – A Head Hunters View   77

CHAPTER 8 – The Job Interview   83

CHAPTER 9 - Soft Skills   93

CHAPTER 10 – FAQ's   99

CHAPTER 11 – A Complete Career Change?   109

CHAPTER 12 - Next steps   115

An Invitation   118

About the author   120

Let's connect   123

Thanks to

*My partner Louise, for her endless encouragement throughout the writing of this book.

*My mum Sheila, for well, being mum. Always there and always supportive.

*Contributors Ian Brodie, Phil Sharp, Rob Brown, and additional insights which I've used in the book from Tony Restell.

*I'm honoured to have the Foreword written by best-selling author of 'The Intuitive Compass' (Best Business Book of the Year USA 2011) Francis Cholle.

*All of my clients, past, present and future. You're all stars, and I continue to learn from you.

*Recruiters who have freely shared their insights into an industry that can often be confusing and frustrating to the outsider. Thanks for sharing your insights.

*Colleagues, new friends and old, and mentors that I have met (many via social media) these past few years. You know who you are.

Foreword

I have heard many entrepreneurs and great corporate leaders say that recruiting is the hardest part of business. Hiring is a necessary and recurring aspect of business. It greatly impacts the probability of success of any organization.

Entering into a new professional relationship is like entering into a marriage. No one wins unless both parties win. Because it involves people's sensitivity, feelings and trust, instinct and intuition should be part of the process of finding a new job.

François-Henri Pinault, CEO of Kering and son of François Pinault, entrepreneur extraordinaire, billionaire and founder of what's become the second French luxury empire, once told me his father had regretted only one recruitment decision he had made. That was the one he did without listening to his instinct....

François' recounting of his father's experience is quite telling. It very much informs how to approach finding a new position. Looking for a new position is a difficult sport to play, and not only for the job seeker, but for both parties involved. This should always be remembered, as it will help any job seeker leave behind unnecessary feelings about oneself or one's candidacy, such as inadequacy, shyness or self-imposition.

Nevertheless, careful preparation matters a lot and requires significant time commitment. Today, online tools such as LinkedIn, Facebook or Twitter are vital platforms to be present on. The essential 'elevator pitch' needs to be advertised in many ways and places. As with any difficult sport, practice makes perfect. But the difficulty lies in practicing the right way. This is where the help of an expert makes a huge difference.

In our increasingly digital world, where relationships unfold under constantly changing circumstances, it is more important than ever for the job seeker to take the lead and read carefully Steve Nicholls' *Reverse Headhunting*. This concise volume is filled with practical tips and actionable recommendations that will help you achieve the career path of your dreams.

Reverse Headhunting is an expert's mapping of all the challenges one faces while searching and the toolbox one needs to win the job market competition.

Francis Cholle
CEO of The Human Company
Best Selling Author of *The Intuitive Compass*

Introduction

Why '*Reverse Headhunting*' as a book title? Essentially because it's ultimately all about networking, about *you* doing the *hunting* (sometimes with a little help perhaps), finding and nurturing those new contacts which so often lead to unearthing those unadvertised or 'hidden' jobs. This book sets out to equip you with insights and strategies to become a successful 'reverse head hunter'.

To begin, a caveat: Many topics surrounding job search, career management, career advice, or career guidance are subjective. Fact. Whatever opinions you seek regarding your CV/Resume, Interview Preparation and more, or how many viewpoints you can absorb, *trust your intuition* as well as your rational side to make informed choices about what works for you in any given situation on your career journey.

This book has been written for senior level executives who are seeking their next role, and while I'm sure there are applicable career lessons right across the seniority spectrum of the jobs market, you should know that some of the points and terminology within will only apply to senior level executives.

From the pages of this book, including the stories, opinion, tips, and ideas; take what works for you, discard the rest. My views are in most cases aligned with feedback received from top level head hunters and those at the sharp end of the recruitment industry, some of whom I've invited to include their views in this book.

My company works with many senior executives across a range of disciplines and sectors; so from our side of the table you tend to pick up on the main concerns, issues, or barriers, with most people on the market for a new role, although some concerns are not always articulated early on in a coaching relationship. This book addresses the most common concerns and 'speed bumps', as well as the processes necessary to engage with the players, to ensure you're as sharp and well informed a candidate as you can be.

Who is this book for? The curious executive job seeker, and those looking for *'that extra 2% or 3%'* in terms of performance potential, which when faced with similarly qualified candidates can be all it comes down to.

When I set out to write this book, I had a very clear idea of who I was writing it for: If you're a senior / board level executive looking for your next role (or looking to progress your career), then it is my intention and hope that you will find value within this book, which has been written as a guide; a pragmatic curriculum of career development learning, which includes tools and strategies for getting that invaluable 'inside track' in today's competitive jobs market. I also hope to bring some additional insights from the so-called 'soft skills' side of the equation, skills which I've found to be underdeveloped in many senior executives.

Working with senior executives has taught me that on the whole a succinct style of communication is normally appreciated, so you will find that parts of this book are extremely to the point, and this is based on having learned what a senior level executive wants/needs to know about a given subject. I like to write as if I am sat across the desk from you, or at the end of a Skype call having a discussion about your own career plans, so I'll try to keep this as conversational as I can.

You may also find your thinking processes and preconceptions challenged along the way; *challenging appropriately* is another key part of my or any coach's role, and one that my clients value, along with support and encouragement of course when the going gets tough.

You'll find chapters on how to improve your *personal branding and why it's important*, how to create a compelling executive level CV/Resume, LinkedIn optimization (and more importantly leveraging the platform), as well as ways to sharpen up your interview skills, especially if you've spent most of the last few years being the interviewer rather than the interviewee.

I have also invited trusted colleagues, including marketing experts and recruiters to offer their views, which I think you'll find invaluable.

You will take away different things from the next person who reads this book, as we all have differing levels of career-related knowledge and needs, some of which, by the way, I have found do not come to light until some way into a coaching relationship, hence it's impossible to recreate every conceivable coaching scenario in the pages of a book; but areas such as confidence, or the lack of, 'blind spots' (which by definition are difficult to identify and acknowledge in ourselves), or just a general sharpening up of skills are some of the common themes that reoccur in conversations I have with many hundreds of people.

So within this book you will find a tool box of resources and ideas for you to dip into as you wish, all of which are designed to give you an edge over other candidates when going for your next senior level role.

How to get the most from this book

What I suggest is that you have a read of the entire book from front to back, soak it all up, then home in on chapters that you think might be of most benefit to you, based on your individual circumstances. If you need further information on any of the areas covered just drop me a line and I'll be more than happy to help. Where ever I am trying to make a point (or perhaps a critical point which is easy to overlook) I will sometimes use italics. Spotting and applying these points will give you that inside track or competitive advantage over other senior level candidates.

At the end of the book there are some pages for you to make notes, so I encourage you to use these and write down action points etc., and then to act on them.

1 - A word on Career Coaching

"Support with your career plans, or 'fly solo'?"

When is the challenge of finding your next role potentially big enough to engage external support such as a career coach? For some not at all, for others it's right at the beginning of their job search, for others it's a few months into their job search, when concerns have grown a little perhaps. Everyone has differing levels of need, support, knowledge, financial 'cushions', and career challenges.

However, it is my business philosophy and overarching mission to offer my knowledge to as many people across the globe as possible, hence writing my first book.

As a coach and as an executive career coaching business, I cannot work with all of you, but it is my passion in life to help senior level executives become the best candidates that they can be, when seeking their next role.

This book is a tool kit for all of you.

Career Coaching & the Career Management industry

This is not a book about career coaching, but I'd like to briefly address the question, "Why work with a career coach and how can they help me?"

I considered not addressing the subject of career coaching at all in this book, but took the view that it might be helpful if I offered my take purely as a bit of a primer about the *career management industry* (sitting as it does between you as a candidate and the recruitment industry), of which I am a part. I will leave it to your judgement whether the input of a professional coach will enhance your career prospects enough to justify your attention and the investment.

The book *is* however about helping you to successfully progress into that next senior role as soon as you desire, at the right salary level and conditions that you require, and part of that equation could be to engage a coach to support you.

But what can a coach bring to the table? What should you expect? First off, ensure that you understand the difference in approaches which are available to you.

Coaching styles and approaches to helping:
Don't get me wrong here; I'm not saying that one style of career coaching or career advice/guidance will yield better results for you than another across the board, but what I

am saying is that you need to ensure that you know what to expect from different approaches, and more importantly whether they match up with your personality and preferred learning style.

What do you need to know? I always advise my clients, or prospective clients to do their *due diligence* before engaging a coach (*see 'top tips for choosing a career coach' in a couple of pages time*). Some general considerations should be:

Are they operating at the right 'level'?
Do you get on with them?
Can you work with them?

(The above are spookily similar questions to those which might be on the mind of the CEO or other Interviewer who might be interviewing you for your next role.)

You may or may not have an understanding where career coaches and career management companies like mine sit in the whole recruitment and job market. I'd like to offer a brief take on this subject as it may *arm you with a few facts*, and things to look out for if you're exploring engaging with a career coach.

First off, it's a fairly mature (although at the time of writing, unregulated) industry, more so than you might think, with some established players operating a varying levels and offering a broad range of services.

When a number of company-wide redundancies or smaller numbers of more senior role losses happen at a company, you may have heard of (or experienced) a so-called 'outplacement' service, which makes it sound like you'll be found another role via the process, but what usually happens is that you'll be taken through a suite of interventions that will attempt to help you in your search for a role (CV, interview skills, et al), but the success of this kind of service can come down to the skill level of the specific coach/consultant who has been allocated to you, and it certainly will not include *proactive marketing* of you to the head hunter and recruitment industry.

At the other end of the coaching continuum (not a scale of expertise or competence mind you) you have the one man band coaches and boutique style organizations, many of whom provide a sterling service, but not all will offer the exact same service, so I return to the subject of due diligence around this subject; ensure that you do yours. I have some top tips which should serve you well if you cover off each point when investigating coaching provision. The updated and expanded version of this list follows:

Some people who are looking for a coach will go by recommendation or word of mouth. Both are fine as far as they go, but coaching is a deeply personal experience, so you need to ensure a *mutual match* across a number of criteria:

Top Tips for choosing a career coach /company

- **Talk, talk, talk!** Most coaches should offer you a complimentary session (usually telephone or Skype), so take advantage of that. Make some notes as you talk to each coach, ready to compare when it comes to deciding. Also see if they have produced any additional content online, so that you can further get a good "feel" for how they work with their clients. Having an initial call is a good opportunity for a "joint discovery" conversation re mutual fit. Importantly here, have they coached people just like you previously?

- **Cost:** This might be at the forefront of your mind, but how willing is the coach to tell you up front (if you ask the question) what their fees are? You should be looking for transparency, and a clear answer. However, view this as an investment in *you*.

- **Added Value:** What kind of follow up does the coach provide? Free email communications between coaching sessions? Limited email? Sector or other specialist knowledge? Anything else that "stands out" for you? Factor in this added value added info to your decision making.
- **Differentiation:** Does the coach offer anything over and above others? It could be a specific offer,

or they might be a "Thought Leader" in their field. This could also be around style of coaching, and will be important when you get to the day-to-day of the coaching relationship. Make a note of anything that differentiates that coach for you.

- **Accreditations/Qualifications:** Again, it varies for different specialisms, but dig a little into where that coach has "come from" – their own work/life experience, and formal accreditations and/or qualifications. Coaching is currently a non-regulated industry, with a few umbrella organizations who are attempting to bring order to the industry. There are many well-meaning coaches out there, but I suggest you look for how they gained their "stripes", and just as importantly, whether they have the experience of helping people like you.

- **Testimonials:** Does the coach have any? Enough said. This could include past clients that you can pick up the phone and have a chat with, or get some feedback from via email, as well as the usual LinkedIn or website testimonials. Your confidence needs to be such that your chosen coaching company or individual has the necessary credibility.
- **Reflect:** Ensure that you have all the facts before making a final choice. This could be a 6+ month's

relationship or longer you're buying into, so you need to be sure. Due diligence is key. Don't rush into any decisions.

- **Rapport:** I'm a great believer in all things *emotional intelligence* as you may quickly have gathered, and the whole subject and importance of *being personable.* When you were speaking with the coach, did it feel comfortable? Did they "get" you? Did you get on? What was your gut feeling telling you? Remember, you will be engaging in many interactions with the coach or coaching organization, so you need to feel the potential to be able to form a good 'business friendship' in a 'trusted advisor' context.

- So the ***bottom line judgement call*** I'd ask you to consider re investigating any form of coaching input is; will it work for you and do you feel it adds enough value to your job hunting strategy?

So let's move on to the meat of this book, starting with the rather self-important sounding subject of "personal branding"...

2 – Personal Branding '101' & Networking

"Thinking Differently. Having Clarity. Being Proactive"

There is so much detailed information and jargon around the whole subject of personal branding, which I intend avoiding, hence the '101' reference in the title. I hope this chapter will give you what you need to know about personal branding in a career planning context.

Like it or not, the subject of *how you package and present yourself as a senior level candidate* (the personal branding piece) IS an important factor (along with growing and nurturing your network, and critically, *proactive marketing*) in today's competitive executive jobs market.

My take on personal branding so far as it relates to a job search, is that it's a catch-all phrase encompassing the various ingredients which go toward making you the best candidate that you can be, and 'owning' what you say to people about yourself.

A lot of this entire concept, and other ideas contained in this book come down to mind set and how much or how little you're prepared to take on new learning, and examine and act on ideas that may be alien to you. In other words, the more open minded you are the more you will gain from this book.

As Morpheus said to Neo in the movie The Matrix, "*Free your mind*"...

The 'Elevator Pitch'

Definition: An elevator pitch, elevator speech, or elevator statement is a short summary used to quickly and simply define a person, profession, product, service, organization or event and its value proposition.

The elevator pitch has been around almost as long as, well, elevators, but remains a necessary step in the armoury of any executive looking for their next role (but equally applies to anyone aspiring to a senior level role). As much as you may like or dislike the phrase itself, see it as a succinct few sentences which sum up your experience and value to the listener.

Some homework: I suggest breaking your basic elevator pitch (yes, there are variances on this one) down into three parts (the context here is always is if you're interacting with a recruiter, head hunter, or someone who can influence recruitment at a company):

1. Intro to you, discipline, sector
2. Value you have brought previously (one or two "knock out punches" (i.e. £$%€ (i.e. financial & other tangible performance results) are ideal here)
3. Aspirational piece – what are you now looking for?

Example of an Elevator Pitch:

'I'm an experienced Chief Financial Officer (insert your main one or two job titles), and I have experience in the xyz and xyz sectors. I have worked on many key projects including one £$€20M example where I reduced overheads by xyz%.
I'm now looking for a challenging new role (you can be specific here regarding. e.g. P&L, size of company – whatever

your own preference or target is) in the xyz sector(s), where I can add value and really make a difference.'

We could of course personally discuss and formulate your own elevator pitch and it might be totally different from the example, but I hope it will give you the broad idea in order to get something written *and rehearsed*. Recording yourself as you practice your elevator pitch can in itself be a lesson in how to vary and use pitch, tone, intonation, inflection and speaking volume.

I would also advise extending this idea to considering an additional elevator pitch around *your top three value-adds that you would bring to a role*. Many a time a senior level candidate has been caught out at an initial meeting or phone call with a recruiter by not having prepared and thought through their various personal branding statements.

For example, imagine you've been invited in for a coffee and a chat with a sector specialist senior level recruiter. You sit down, having just placed your cup of tea/coffee on the table after the first sip, and they say to you, *"So Steve, thanks for coming in. What are your three key areas of value that you would bring to a new role?"* Wow! Were you prepared for that question? I hope so, as this scenario can happen more often than you might think.

What I'm advocating of course here is to be fully prepared and *on top of your game* well in advance. So taking that example I would suggest another piece of homework;

Write your three keys selling points (differentiators or value-adds), around 30 seconds each in duration, practice and polish them, and be ready for this type of question. This piece of work will be one of your two core elevator pitches, along with the more general 'intro style' elevator pitch.

Networking

Many senior executives that I speak with hold a view that their networking skills are below par, along with the fact that embarking on this particularly activity is one which gives them the same sinking feeling as having to attend a dental appointment!

Of course there are skills involved in networking, but some of the ability comes simply from the fact that extraverts find the whole process easier than introverts. I'll aim most of this section at those who are looking for a few tips and pointers to make the whole networking activity easier.

Trusted colleagues will be offering their input within this chapter also.

It's not all about you. Stephen Covey anyone? (Yes, I'm talking about adopting a *win-win* approach as outlined in his book *The 7 Habits of Highly Effective People*). Your initial and ongoing networking mind-set should be one of trying to *give value and support as well as receive it*, whether from a peer to peer meeting, or with a recruiter: *This is so key that once you "get it" it will take your networking to another level.*

LinkedIn Networking

I asked my friend and colleague, marketing expert Ian Brodie of www.ianbrodie.com to give me his take on networking your way toward your next role via LinkedIn (a subject which I'll cover further in a later chapter, as it's such a vital; component of the networking mix).

Ian has been regularly voted one of the top global influencers on the subject of marketing, so he's worth listening to:

My main brief to Ian was to ask him to provide concrete, actionable tips around LinkedIn:

Ian says; It's difficult to move these days without being told by one expert or another that we MUST be active on social media. But the truth is that most highly active social media users get very little from it other than a warm fuzzy feeling that somehow in some way they're building their profile.

For a busy executive with huge demands on their time and energy, that's not enough. You need to focus your attention on high payoff activities that make a real impact and deliver results.

Here are three simple, interlinked strategies you can follow on LinkedIn that have been shown time and time again to deliver tangible value:

The first is to make your profile "customer focussed".

Whether you're an active user of LinkedIn or not, it's inevitable these days that before meeting or speaking with you, most people in business are going to check out your LinkedIn profile.

Many executives still have a blank or abbreviated profile with just a few short lines. Or worse, they've filled their profile but with content that's irrelevant or actually off-putting for the people they most want to see it.

When you join LinkedIn it starts off by asking about your previous employment roles and education. The implication is that LinkedIn is an online CV or résumé and most people take that at face value and treat it as such. So their profile is all about their job achievements, how many people they've managed, the budgets they've controlled.

The problem is, that's not necessarily interesting or useful to the people reading your profile.

When you create your LinkedIn profile, particularly the summary where you can control exactly what appears in it; make it "customer focused".

In other words, think through who the ideal person for you to read this profile would be and design it for them.

If your goal is to network with other executives, then make sure your profile focuses on the things that would make other executives interested in connecting with you. If your goal is to create the right impression with board members who could be future employers, then make sure your profile talks about the sort of strategic and bottom-line achievements that board members are likely to be interested in.

You have complete control over what appears in your profile summary, and it's the primary thing most people looking at your profile will read. So devote time to crafting one that will create the right impression with the people you're most looking to connect with.

The second strategy is to connect wisely.

On LinkedIn you'll find some people who seem to collect connections like stamps. They have thousands of connections, yet don't build real relationships with any of them. They're the LinkedIn equivalents of those awful networkers you sometimes meet at events who push their business cards into everyone's hands yet never take the time to engage with anyone or follow up.

Others only connect with people on LinkedIn who they already know face-to-face. That's like the people at events who hang around in their existing cliques and never make any new contacts.

The people on LinkedIn who tend to get the most from it are the ones who connect wisely. They make sure that they're harnessing their existing network (we'll see how to do that in the next strategy), but they also accept and look for connections with new contacts who are well connected or who could be clients or hirers themselves.

But they don't stop at connecting with them. Just like if you meet someone interesting who could be a valuable contact at a face-to-face event: you follow-up.

So if you connect with someone or they offer to connect with you, follow-up with a message afterwards. Check out their profile and look for areas of commonality to highlight.

If it looks like they could be a valuable connection, follow up again within a week with a question, or to send them something you think they might find useful based on your initial interactions (a link to an article for example, or an event they might want to attend).

Go for a smaller number of quality connections, and actively nurture those relationships. That way if you need to ask a favour you won't be asking cold.

The final strategy is to harness your network for referrals.

We all know the best way of connecting with a potential client or a board member who might hire you in future is to get a personal introduction. Unfortunately, those introductions rarely happen spontaneously.

Asking for referrals proactively can be a powerful strategy, and it's one you'll be advised to follow time and time again.

But getting results from a proactive referral strategy isn't as easy as it sounds. What most people do is ask their contacts very generally: "if you know anyone who…".

Of course, none of us knows "anyone". That's too vague and it's asking us to do all the hard work for you.

What's much better is to ask for introductions to specific people. That way the people you ask don't have to think about it. They just need to say yes or no.
Asking for specific introductions used to be restricted to the rare occasions when you spotted your contact talking to someone you wanted to meet, or they mentioned them in conversation. Typically we're not really that aware of who our contacts know.

But thanks to LinkedIn, we can now get deep visibility of our contacts' networks (unless they decide to make their network invisible of course, in which case you'll only see 'common' connections).

You can either just browse the list of contacts of the people you're connected with looking for interesting people to ask for referrals to (focus on the contacts you're confident know you well enough to be willing to introduce you). Or you can use LinkedIn's advanced search facility to search for people who meet the exact criteria of person you're looking to meet (for example by searching for their job title, industry, geography or seniority).

Once you've spotted great people to be introduced to, you can ask for that specific introduction from your contacts. And by asking for specific names you're much more likely to get an introduction than the traditional generic request.

If you use all three of these strategies, they work in harmony.

Having a "customer focused" profile means the people you ask for introductions to are more likely to say yes to connecting with and meeting with you. Building strategic connections and following up to nurture your relationships means your contacts are much more likely to be willing and motivated to help you and introduce you to their best contacts.

And getting referrals to the exact people you're interested in meeting: that's gold dust.

Thanks to Ian for that input, and following this, where does it leave face to face networking?

Is Face to Face networking still necessary?

Many job candidates focus on the 'remote' or web-based aspects of networking, especially nowadays when the emphasis seems highly skewed toward social networks and their undoubted power, which I'm certainly not disputing. But it's only part of the story.

So what is the relevance of face-to-face networking today?

I spoke with Rob Brown, bestselling author of the book 'How to Build Your Reputation'. Rob is a global authority on building and leveraging powerful networks.

Here are some of his top tips for 'working a room' and networking more productively.

- **Survey the Room**

Don't just rush into it. Take a few moments to survey the room. Grab a (non-alcoholic) drink if necessary, to give you the excuse to stand back and look at what's happening. Remind yourself why you are there, who you want to see and why, and look for anyone you may know who you really want to speak to. Then select the individuals or open groups to approach – more on that later.

- **2. Stay in Control**

If you can't stick to the fruit juice or water, don't overdo it on the alcohol! One drink might calm your nerves, but more than that and your brain will begin to feel the effects. Best to stick to the water!

- **Keep Focussed**

Even if you get into a very good chat and are having a great time, don't use that as an excuse to really chase the contacts that might result in potential new roles. You could make lots of friends, but they might be people who can't help you get your next job. Don't ignore anyone, but stay targeted on those who are likely to help you achieve your goals for the event.

- **Be Positive**

As someone once said, get yourself in the right state of mind, not in a right state! When you enter the room, keep your head up, shoulders back, smile and look as if networking is like falling off a log. If you're nervous – don't show it – but be assured that the majority of people in the room feel just the same as you.

- **Be Interested in Others**

The phrase 'working a room' sounds rather aggressive and self-seeking, but remember that sustainable networking success is not about exploitation but building relationships *for mutual benefit*. If you are pushy and launch into elevator pitches before you've established a relationship, you'll soon be shunned at networking events. And if you have no conversations, you'll have no relationships, no opportunities and no new contacts. So make sure you are more interested in helping than pitching, and doing more listening than talking.

- **6. Be Patient**

Building relationships through networking is a long-term game. New contacts are unlikely to spill the beans on all their needs until they've got to know you, trust you and understand what you have to offer. Besides, they might not have a suitable role right now (assuming it's a gathering of head hunters and recruiters) – but they may have in six months' time. So the aim is to get to know people, and get them to know you, so when they do have a need you are 'front of mind' and the first one they come to. That's why maintaining relationships at networking events is just as important as meeting new people.

- **7. Approach Strangers**

You can't be a wallflower. You have to be pro-active to be a networker. Don't worry, strangers expect to be approached. This is a networking event, after all.

- **8. Be Polite**

Those little words like 'please', 'thank you' and 'excuse me' make a big difference. If you are rude or inconsiderate, you won't win many friends – and people only do business with their friends, not with their enemies.

- **9. Know How to Exit**

If you're feeling trapped and bored in a conversation, guess what the other person is feeling? Don't prolong the agony for either of you. Be the first to make a move, and exit your conversation graciously. One way to do this is by inviting them to get a drink or some food with you. In the process of moving to the drinks or food table, you may bump into other people on the way and naturally begin talking to others. Alternatively, express your apologies and say you've spotted someone you promised to speak to and you don't want to let them down. Then thank the person for talking with you, say it was nice to meet them, and leave.

- **10. Use Your Questions**

Great questions lead to great conversations, which lead to great relationships, which lead to great opportunities. It's one of my favourite sayings, because it works. Having already prepared some questions, make sure you use them to develop the small talk, then gradually introduce some about their business, then their issues or needs.

Rob says, 'Business is personal, and even the biggest deals, orders, projects, sales, promotions and contracts come down to two or more people making a connection.' That can also apply to the recruitment process.

Some great advice there from Rob, but what should you do next? My advice would be to track down a local networking event and put some of these tips into action. It doesn't necessarily need to be a meeting with recruiters, but could be a peer networking event. Just 'get in there', take that deep breath and practice. That's a challenge for you (especially if networking isn't your 'thing') perhaps, but go for it, and let me know how you get on. One other tip would be to get some personal business cards printed, with your name, email, contact number, and LinkedIn (and other social media) ID purely for these events, as well as the inevitable 'coffee meetings' which will happen during your job search.

3 – The CV / Resume

The subject of the humble CV/Resume is as likely to start a lively debate as any discussion around politics or world peace! There are many CV/Resume opinions, and 'the right way to do it' views out there, and like I always say it's your own due diligence around discussing your options (particularly if going down the path of engaging a professional CV writer) which will ensure you end up with a document that's going to work for you and get read and acted upon by a recruiter, and in the end that's all that matters.

The Curriculum Vitae or Resume (I'll use the acronym CV going forward) is the cornerstone of any personal branding piece, and forms the foundation of your creation of a 'personal brand', which you will present to the recruitment market when you are ready. It's the first point of contact for most candidate / recruiter relationships, aside from social media which will only continue to become more important. However, the humble CV still has life in it, and in my opinion will continue to be around for some time to come in one form or another.

My views of what makes a good executive level CV are informed from my own experience, and importantly, what I have learned from a great many recruiters and head hunters during conversations I've had with them, when I always ask questions such as, "What do you normally look at first on a CV?", "What do you like to see on a senior level CV?".

So yes the CV is a subjective topic, and you have to apply what works for you. The advice that follows will provide the means to create a strong executive level CV template, but remember it is just that, a template which can be adjusted based on the requirements of any given role. Many recruiters will want to re-write your CV based on a specific role in any case.

Problems with CV's

People often tell me the main concerns they have about their CV are:

- Too many opinions about what makes a good CV

- Not getting enough interviews

- Difficult to get skills and value across to the reader

- How to get recruiters to take notice of the CV

So to take those points one at a time:

Opinions, opinions!

As I've suggested there are many styles of CV, but after many and frequent discussions with senior level head hunters and recruiters, the style that I recommend is one which is based on their majority feedback. I am also constantly updating my knowledge in this area, by having regular dialogue with top level head hunters and recruiters in the industry.

Although you'll hear many compelling arguments and standpoints around this subject, a simply formatted, easy to read CV is what is required 90+% of the time when I ask this question of recruiters, who are in effect the gate keepers for their clients, so they haven't got time to be interpreting anything on your CV. It needs to be sharp, to the point, and have a few 'knock out punches' as I call them, i.e. strong achievement points including relevant £$%€ information if appropriate.

Lack of Interviews? Use this style of CV:

Not getting enough interviews? What I propose as a core CV template style is simple; *a compelling* (and I use the word *compelling* intentionally) *executive summary (which you may know as the personal profile section at the top of page one) followed by the chronological career history – most recent role first.* It's a straightforward layout, without any fancy formatting. There are a few subtleties around getting this right, but essentially that's the style I recommend. This will, I believe, get you more interest and interviews. Let's break it down:

How to write a compelling 'Executive Summary'

For the executive summary, it should be around 6-10 lines long, and as punchy as possible. Yes just 6-10 lines. It's a summary; that is all, and needs to be compelling enough to grab attention of the recruiter or employer in a short space of time. Lose as many adjectives as you can, and focus on what you can bring to the market. This succinctness is not only appreciated, but is expected at senior level. It's also useful to get some £$%€ info included in the summary as well, as recruiters eyes are drawn to this type of information.

At the very end of the executive summary, you can also include an aspirational piece around specific discipline and sector required in your next role.

State your case and keep it simple; reduce adjectives where possible. I would also suggest "*person*-neutrality" in your description, so e.g. "A commercially astute (CEO, CFO, MD, Finance Director Etc.)...", rather than "*I am* a commercially astute....etc". Again, it just helps to keep things 'high level'.

It's worth taking some time to refine this executive summary and to invite critiques from trusted advisers, as it's often (but not always, read on...) the first thing that a recruiter will read from your CV. Your previously prepared elevator pitch could have something to add to the executive summary, so you can refer back to that, flesh things out a bit more, and you will be well on your way to constructing a summary that sells you to the reader.

Adding impact to your career history

With each company that you have worked for, aside from the relevant dates, I suggest you include one or two lines just under the company name describing the size and nature of the organization. Assuming you are going for a clear type face like 11pt. Arial or Calibri for example for the main body of the CV this company description would be in 9pt. italics, e.g. *xyz company is a £500M turnover company specializing in the production of xyz, employing over 300 staff.* This helps the recruiter or HR person to quickly see the types of companies you have worked for; you're actively helping the reader by having this additional information.

As far as the chronological career history section is concerned, *(which is the other key area a recruiter's eye may be drawn to initially)* assuming you're using a bullet point style breakdown of key achievements, these points need to have significant *results* described... "I was a board member, and contributed to various aspects of company business" is not enough in a competitive jobs market.

The *results* could be around 'EBITDA' info, P&L, % reduction in attrition rates, or improvements in company culture or processes (human impact), and so on. It's always good to get some hard facts, percentages, or figures in each bullet point, but only if it is relevant to your discipline and sector, but it most often will be for senior level candidates.

It's worth outlining the *STAR CV Format* here, also known by other acronyms which essentially cover the same steps toward a logical sequence of describing your achievements *(also handy to bear in mind as a process for answering interview questions).*

The STAR CV Format overview

S is for Situation. Rather than simply launching into any given bullet point on your CV, even if you detail the result, is the *context* or backdrop relevant to the point. Remember, someone has to read and 'get' each and every point on your CV without thinking too hard about it. E.g. 'Against a backdrop of poor performance in xyz...' helps the reader to form a picture, a flow if you will, of the entire situation.

T is for Task. Ok, so you had (as above) the hypothetical situation of poor performance in a certain division/department perhaps, so when you metaphorically sat back and thought, 'Right, *this* is what I need to do to rectify this', what was that task? Describe the (T)ask you set yourself to correct the situation. This would be just the high level description of the task itself.

A is for Action. So you decided what the task(s) ahead of you was regarding the hypothetical situation in the 'S' of star, above. Now here's your chance to outline the actual steps you took to resolve the situation as part of that action. You may have introduced new methods of working or process improvements, analysed budgets, introduced new working practices, for example.

R is for Result. What *tangible result* was achieved by the steps taken in the points 1-3 above? Below I have detailed an example of a point before and after the STAR format has been applied (normally via individual discussion with clients, but you can run through your own CV bullet points to test this).

Example Bullet point pre STAR format:

'I controlled various diverse departments and reported to the board on all financial areas of the business'.

Example Bullet point post STAR format (this following example would normally be agreed following a discussion of course):

Joining the company during challenging times, I was tasked with improving the profit area within the xyz division. I created streamlined reporting systems and clear goals, resulting in an improvement of %£$€ within 6 months.

Which of these examples has more impact, and better explains what you did and how you did it?

Nevertheless, you will also see that applying the star format can extend any given bullet's length point to the stage where you may start to think you're going to have the longest CV ever! Initially the CV will indeed lengthen, but with some astute formatting, editing and examination of each and every bullet point (i.e. should they all stay?

Should some be merged?), you will find that it will 'settle' in terms of volume after a few drafts.

In terms of overall length, don't be overly obsessed by the two page 'rule' which seems to be popular among some in the CV writing industry. I find that typically, a senior executive is going to find it extremely restrictive to limit him/herself to a 2 page document. For most people that we work with, a CV around 3 pages is perfectly fine. There can be cultural and country variations re CV practices; in some countries, a photo is advisable, or stating marital status, and in other cases a succinct one page cover sheet often goes down well with recruiters. What works best will depend where you're living and more importantly if you're looking for a country move, then the preferred style of that country should be adopted.

Personal branding; getting your CV noticed by recruiters

As far as your personal branding is concerned, the CV is *the* fundamental linchpin in the entire piece. Following the above processes will give your CV more of a chance of being noticed by recruiters if you apply the ideas, but also depends on how well you have differentiated yourself to the reader. This is also about getting you onto the "read later" pile, rather than being binned (or the electronic equivalent of these options).

How to prepare for a recruiter interview?

Positioning yourself with confidence - your elevator pitch(es)

Let's assume for a moment that you have created a storming CV, and if you were to be teleported Star Trek style, right now, to the offices of a head hunter in order to discuss a role that you were well suited to, who then asked you right in the middle of your first sip of coffee *"So, tell me Steve, what are you about and what are you looking for?"*, would you be able to confidently and clearly articulate your background and experience together with an idea of what you are seeking in a new role, without confusing the person, or boring them to death by rambling on?

Having at least one, but I recommend two elevator pitches, that you can pull out of the bag when you need them. *This is a crucial step* along the path of building your credibility as being a strong candidate for any role that you might go for.

Like many things, these elevator pitches don't necessarily come easily. It takes time. It takes practice, but regardless of how busy you are, making time to do this can result in tangible gains. I described an outline structure earlier in the book for an elevator pitch, and I strongly suggest that you role play (speaking aloud) your answers to this type of question. Articulating your pitch, or interview answers aloud allows you to refine and hone what you want to say, and simply to get used to the sound of your own voice in relation to the interview process.

So, get that CV honed, but align this with preparation to 'walk the talk', as you may not get much chance to prepare for a recruiter or head hunter conversation, whether face to face or on the telephone.

4 - The Hidden Jobs Market

"I know that ideal job is here somewhere".

You will probably have heard of the so-called "hidden jobs market" (HJM). Is it a fact or Myth? Well, in my view it's a bit of both, hence my "so called" reference.

I started looking at this phenomenon a couple of years ago, and discovered some very interesting data. The USA-based research I discovered basically showed that 'the number of new jobs secured was not mirroring the number of job vacancies advertised in the way it had historically done' - so the proportion of all jobs that are "hidden" (unadvertised) has risen with the advent of LinkedIn, employer referral schemes, more aggressive talent retention strategies, and entire in-house recruitment teams. Something like 70-80% of all jobs are unadvertised (i.e. hidden), so it's something worth looking into a bit further to say the least.

I think this pattern / balance is undoubtedly here to stay – from a recruiters perspective new technologies have made it less costly to directly approach a shortlist of desirable candidates without ever posting a job vacancy, it follows that more roles will therefore be filled this way, but it can be a lot of hard work as a candidate to navigate all of this.

Here are 3 tips to help make the HJM work for you:

1. Know exactly who the key players are and connect with them. (I'm referring to LinkedIn and other social media when I say "connect") You might have already realised I'm a bit of a LinkedIn evangelist!

2. Have an effective social media profile (I'm referring to a consistent approach across all platforms, focused on what those key players need to see to get the right impression).

3. Reach out proactively and regularly to establish connections with the key players; recruiters, 2nd degree connections, and leaders in companies you would like to work for. Use LinkedIn groups and other social media platforms to connect with these people.

The phrase *hidden jobs* (or unadvertised jobs) refers to those jobs that never come on to the open market, as they are filled by someone usually saying to a contact, "Do you know anyone who might suit this assignment we're working on...?" (We get these calls from recruiters regularly).

Of course, internally filled posts come under the umbrella of the HJM and form a slice of the cake, but when some in my industry (the career management industry) refer to the HJM & imply that you as a candidate won't have ready access to head hunters and recruiters in the same way as those, like myself, in the industry do, they're only right to some extent. While you may not have the database, you do have the access – **via social networking and the web!**

While many coaching organizations will have head hunter contacts, that doesn't mean *you* cannot pick up the phone and cold call or email a new head hunter or recruiter about a role (or to simply register your availability) in the same way as I would. However you may not feel comfortable doing this, but it's worth taking that "brave pill" and jumping into this activity.

So, I return to my point: the process of scheduling a number of daily regular calls to the appropriate level of head hunter and recruiter *is* something that you *could* do... if you chose to, or *have the time*, which sometimes but not always depends whether you're in a role currently or not.

The HJM can seem to be a nightmare for most people to navigate, but again I would emphasise it's not impossible.

You just need the time and right approach, to engage the recruiters and head hunters on a regular basis.

Remember, we're talking the lion's share of roles – 70-80% being "hidden"…

Ensure that you have a disciplined on-going daily LinkedIn connection strategy for starters. This means connecting with relevant recruiters and then engaging in a dialogue, *not necessarily just pushing your CV to them straight away*. Take a moment to understand the recruiter, and it can pay off.

Connecting with relevant peers can also be a good idea in terms of networking and letting key people know that you're on the market.

Yes, this whole engagement process is still a *numbers game* to some degree (so you cannot expect to call 2 new contacts a week and have something major happen as a result (well, you might get lucky!), and I know there are always exceptions), but demonstrating you're prepared to pick up the phone and call for example is something recruiters actually like.

There is a caveat with the approach I suggest here. A head hunter mentioned to me recently that his industry only deals with a relatively small percentage of roles compared to the whole market, so the HJM is not just about connecting with recruiters, but also with 2nd degree connections and beyond, and direct company approaches works well for some people.

So yes, you *can* gain access to the HJM yourself by active networking until you find the right role. That's as simply as I can put it. But I want to close with a warning...

I'm on my Soapbox!

Don't be put off by some of the hype in some areas of the career management industry that you might hear regarding the HJM and how "Only trained professionals can navigate this area" and some company claims that that *"Without their network of recruiters and head hunters, and their access to unadvertised roles you will be struggling"*. This sales pitch is merely a justification for charging you bloated fees, so beware. With a concerted effort and a battle plan, navigating the hidden jobs market is something you can start doing. Today.

That's just my little soapbox piece about *some elements* of the career management industry, which I always like to let candidates know about. I feel proud to be part of the career management industry, but it's important that you know about some of the potential pitfalls and sales tactics.

To return to the HJM, there are other important issues around accessing it: Establish a credible personal brand first, which is consistent across all platforms (including social media and your CV/Resume). There's little point in having a CV or LinkedIn profile that doesn't reflect your value properly, and then at the same time marketing yourself to the recruitment industry, so get these elements right first before moving onto marketing yourself.

'Takeaways' from this chapter

1. Pro activity is key. Having a good looking, well thought out LinkedIn profile is one thing, but you need to get amongst people, connect and start conversations to unlock the HJM.

2. Record and track: whether you use a spread sheet, LinkedIn's own "reminder" system, or a CRM system ensure that you track conversations you've been having.

3. Direct approaches: don't underestimate this style of speculative application. Only 10-20% of all roles are filled via recruiters, with most coming via 2nd level contacts or via a direct approach to a company.

5 – LinkedIn Revisited & other social media

"Connecting with peers as well as appropriate head hunters and recruiters can bring surprising results".

I've talked a bit about LinkedIn in the personal branding chapter, but I want to drill a bit deeper into the profile itself and more importantly, *how to leverage it to your advantage,* as well as reasons why LinkedIn may not be working for you. I'm going to focus on LinkedIn as the key online networking tool for your next role, although following this piece I will move on to cover a couple of others, specifically Google + and Twitter. I know that there are many who gain traction from Twitter, but a high percentage of our clients are much more concerned about how to get LinkedIn working for them, so that will be my focus for this chapter.

Over the past few years LinkedIn has become much more prevalent as a networking tool with a sophisticated, highly remunerated membership numbering in the hundreds of millions. Nevertheless, I'm convinced that most senior level candidates are not using the platform to best effect. Make no mistake, if you're not using LinkedIn as a serious job hunting tool, and when in your next role, as a networking tool, you are missing a massive trick! Take a deep breath, perhaps also take a 'brave pill' as one of my clients used to describe it, and start to allocate some regular time to LinkedIn specifically using it as a networking and marketing tool.

There are literally a virtual 'ton' of articles written about LinkedIn; how to optimise your profile, attract more visitors etc., so what I intend doing in this chapter is to focus on how senior level candidates specifically can gain benefits from taking a bit of time to not only get their profile right, but to get to the real 'juice'; *proactive, but often subtle (read non pushy) marketing.*

Yes, for LinkedIn to really work for you, an investment of your time is highly recommended, and is really the only way that you will achieve the results that are possible. I suggest an hour or two a day will suffice.

That piece of advice will hopefully remain relevant as the years roll on, as one thing is sure, LinkedIn does like to change things, and 'move the goal posts' from time to time, making it difficult for the average user to keep abreast of the menu systems, and how to really make the best use of the service. We train people on how to get the best out of LinkedIn, and still have problems keeping up from time to time!

Your LinkedIn Profile

Let's get some of the basics covered, enabling you to build a profile that will attract the attention of a recruiter who might be searching for a candidate with your background and experience. Putting in an hour or two to this activity can make a significant difference to your networking efforts. This section cannot cover everything there is to know about LinkedIn; one LinkedIn employee told me that he could "talk for days" about the various features of LinkedIn, so I intend focussing on the bits that are going to support your job search the most.

CV importing

I don't advocate uploading your CV to your profile, a feature which is of course available. The reason I advise this is that a CV can change and evolve over time, and you want to concentrate your efforts on nurturing relationships and starting conversations; then submitting your CV. What I suggest is to extract the key career bullet points and slot those into the main career history section in your LinkedIn profile, while appreciating that some information will be confidential, but you may still allude to specific improvements or achievements.

Photo

I've seen some poor examples of LinkedIn profile photos. Perhaps some downright funny or odd ones too. Rather than listing some strange examples I've seen examples for comic effect, can I just say a standard business headshot, head and shoulders, in business attire is the safest and for senior level the most appropriate to go for. LinkedIn lets you use a decent resolution photograph nowadays also, so take advantage of this and use as high a quality shot as you can.

Headline

There are a couple of popular approaches with creating the headline, which gives you quite a few characters to play with incidentally, at the time of writing.

The first approach is to state that you're *seeking a new role*, e.g. 'Finance Director with significant experience in xyz sector now seeking fresh challenge' or similar. This does a couple of things: first it clearly states your role / discipline and sector experience, which is what a recruiter seeking candidates will be typing into the search box (among other terms dependant on the role in question). Yes, there's another view which sees this approach as looking 'desperate'. For me, it has to be comfortable for you and reflect how you want to be presented to the virtual world.

The second approach is if you are perhaps still in a role, and hence your job search needs to be a discrete one. You can still essentially put the title and sector that you're in without creating an obvious message, e.g. 'CEO with significant PE experience, currently working in xyz sector'. This approach still means you can be found by a recruiter seeking someone with your background and expertise.

Summary Section

Think of this section as being similar to the executive summary on your CV, but not exactly... What some people miss is that you can afford to be a bit more personable. Show a bit more of your brand, if you will, which your CV would not allow you to do. I would add to the general summary a few of the 'knockout punch' bullet points from your CV, but again I understand that this is only possible if you're engaged in an open search rather than a discrete one.

Keywords are a crucial element of being found on LinkedIn, and most people ignore them. I advocate ensuring that any keywords that are important to you, are listed in your headline, most recent role, and that your skills and endorsements section is also strong; it's all about getting *found* over and above your peers through selective keyword placement.

Career history and most recent role

I usually advise people to mention that they are seeking a new role if this is possible, following a redundancy situation or 'garden leave' perhaps (i.e. date it accordingly as a new 'role'). It gives one less thing to have to explain to a recruiter or potential employer. Part of your confident personal brand *elevator pitch* would be to explain the circumstances, and that you're taking your time, seeking the right role, without rushing into it.

Now I know that this may appear to be bullishness over reason, but I'd prefer you to be confident, bordering on bullish, than being the eager puppy, so to speak. So if you've been seeking a new role for 6 months, say so. It's quite common for a senior level role to take 6 months and sometimes much longer for some very senior roles.

I remember feeling fairly put out when LinkedIn introduced endorsements. All of a sudden there we all were, having to create a list of seemingly random "skills" with various connections (whether they know we can deliver on any given skill or not) randomly "ticking" skills, and so over time a *top ten* would appear, and it's difficult to influence the order of that top ten and beyond, aside from actively asking contacts to endorse you for certain skills, in order to influence the top ten into something resembling your *actual* skills. But this section is here to stay by all accounts, so we have to work with it, but it's debatable if this section influences how "findable" you are for each specific key word you've listed, although most of my sources indicate it is an influencer in your search rankings.

This is LinkedIn's *official* take on Skills and Endorsements:

- **Make your endorsements count:** It's important to be thoughtful about what skill you endorse. We encourage you to focus on skills and expertise you can personally attest to or have experienced first-hand. If you think your connection is being too humble for their own good, suggest a skill they may not have listed yet on their profile. Just remember, the endorsee must accept the suggested skill before it appears on their profile.

- **Reach out and reconnect:** Use this as an opportunity to keep in touch with your network. When you visit a connection's profile page, you may see a module up top suggesting relevant skills you can endorse. Use this as an opportunity to reconnect with an old connection by endorsing them for work you've done together at your last company. Don't see the skill you had in mind? Just "X" out the suggested one and type in the skill you'd like to recommend.

- **Show off your best assets:** You have full control of what endorsements and endorsers show up on your profile. Perhaps you want to show only notable connections in your industry who've endorsed you for a particular skill. Simply go to "manage endorsements" to select specific endorsements or endorsers you'd like shown or not shown. We've also added the ability to hide all your Endorsements if you prefer not to have any endorsements on your profile.

- **Make your endorsements work for you:** Say you're making a career switch or looking for specific kinds of business opportunities. You have the ability to show off select skills and endorsements on your profile by simply going to "edit" mode on your profile. Click on the pencil icon next to the skills and expertise section, and quickly add or remove skills from your profile. Voila! Only the skills and endorsements you think best represent who you are or want to be professionally will be shown on your LinkedIn profile *(Author's note: You can now 're-order' your endorsements, if you think that certain skills that you want to promote more are not getting the 'clicks' you'd like).*

So that's what LinkedIn says. For now, Skills and Endorsement are here to stay, but I would not ignore them or be too cynical about them. Imagine what a recruiter or employer *might* think if you had no endorsements and a competitor for a role had lots of them? Sounds like a bit of a guessing game? Yes it is, but we have to play the game so I suggest *watching this space* re endorsements.

Voluntary work section

People that you connect with as well as potential employers often like the fact that you are involved in some form of charitable efforts. If you are, then outline your work in this section.

But whatever you do, perhaps LinkedIn just isn't working for you? Read on for tips on how to gain more traction:

Possible reasons why LinkedIn is not working for you

- The goal posts are always being moved

There are times when I log into LinkedIn only to find that, "Hello, they've changed that menu, or this option, or that service has now become a premium option...etc". Hence it's tough for the casual user to keep tabs on how the changes can benefit or hinder a job search. I train people in using LinkedIn, and I sometimes struggle to keep pace, so I appreciate what it can be like to the average user.

- Most candidates see LinkedIn as a passive tool

You can do your bit to attract more profile views by raising your own profile and visibility by being proactive within groups or via your own feed if groups aren't your thing (but you're missing out if you take this approach) - "liking" a post, commenting on someone else's post, posting something *of interest* yourself. Do these things and you will see more visits to your profile.

So, into the meat of getting LinkedIn to work for you...

How to decide which groups to use? – This is KEY, as it's the main way that you will gain access to the HJM...

At the time of writing (remember LinkedIn likes to change things) on every group there is an italicized *i* (information & settings) to the top right hand side. Click on that and you will see a black panel with blue/white text. Under the ABOUT heading click on statistics... You will see headings for:

Summary
Demographics
Growth
Activity

I suggest you have a look around at these various stats, have a play, and see if the membership is aligned with what you're looking for – *Demographics* is a good one to begin with, which you will then see it gives you access to further data: SENIORITY, FUNCTION, LOCATION, INDUSTRY. So, I think you'll see there's a bit of research you can do to establish whether a group is likely to be potentially interesting or useful before you jump in.

After you've taken the plunge and joined a few (or a few more) groups

1. Observe – even though you've done a bit of due diligence... (See what's being posted / discussed)
2. "Like" – this will appear in your feed and others you're connected to
3. Comment – e.g. "Hi John, I found what you said interesting. Have you heard of... etc. (*Ask a question*. This is good for generating a discussion)
4. Post something of interest yourself (and add your views, then ask a question)

Let's look at *why* you're doing all of these things: you will discover that more people – it could be peers, ex colleagues, recruiters – doesn't really matter who it is for now – will start to check you out. If a recruiter looks at your profile though, what would you normally do? Well, if you're not all over it like a rash, I would suggest that's the best action; either pick up the phone or email them immediately. They may have looked at your profile, not seen what they were looking for, and moved on... a call can help explain that perhaps you DO have what they were looking for. This pro-activity and fast action is called for, or you could easily miss the boat as far as that particular potential role is concerned.

Returning to group activity, if you just cannot bring yourself to start posting, commenting or engaging within groups, then there's another strategy which might suit you:

Connect strategically

Most senior executives have taken a careful and measured approach to their career, and can be extremely cautious when it comes to self-promotion or networking of any sort. I understand this completely, so what I'm advocating is a systematized method for joining the "right" groups, and then starting to "dip your toe in the waters" of participation within those groups.

So, I think you'll see there's a bit of research you can do to establish whether a group is likely to be potentially interesting or appropriate before you jump in. just ensure that you do the due diligence exercise I suggested a couple of pages ago.

The next step would be to observe what the interactions are like in the group. Who are the movers and shakers? Is it a "spammy" type of group? (Endless promotional postings with no real engagement or interaction among members) I used to say at this stage "Get out!" if it is a spammy group, but before you go down this route perhaps it's worth having a look at the 2nd degree connections? There could be plenty of people, like you, you have joined a group and not bothered to leave. These could be useful connections for your job search or future networking.

Once you've decided a LinkedIn group is right for you

If it seems like a good group for you to be involved in, start by clicking "like" on one or two posts of interest, then progress to leaving an answer or two to a suitable post. The final step here would be to post an article of interest (you can link to it), or open with a question of potential interest to peers, or other senior professionals (do you notice I'm not talking *just* about recruiters here). Now imagine this new activity replicated across a number of groups. *Can you see how this might generate interest in you?* But only if you take action, and continue to take action until your objectives are achieved.

These strategies are for leveraging LinkedIn rather than just being passive about the whole process. It will require effort, and a plan, so I suggest you commit to an hour a day initially to get things running, then you can also focus on some face to face networking (a whole other subject, but an important one).

Since the introduction of the *publishing platform* (accessible via the 'pencil' icon on your LinkedIn home page), those that I have suggested use it seem to be getting more shares and 'likes' than promoting their own blog for example, so it seems like a powerful feature, and I'd suggest giving it a try.

Other Social media

Google+

Who knows the 'underground' workings of Google algorithms? Who cares, I hear you say! Well, there is a reason to have a presence on Google+, even though you may not be that proactive with the platform. It's all about search rankings. I have to qualify this as anecdotal, but it seems that (as you might expect) Google search itself 'likes' Google+. So, the reason you'd want a Google+ presence is to help your actual rankings under Google search. One quick tip: Post often and get those +1's. +1's are Google's way of identifying and thereby indexing what it sees as popular content. The more +1's you have, the more Google thinks your content is relevant and the better rankings you will get. If you're an avid blogger or you post content, or share content via LinkedIn, you can also share the content to Google+.

Twitter

Until relatively recent times I didn't have too much time for Twitter. It seemed to 'light', too transient to be seen as a useful tool for executive job search. Owner of www.social-hire.com, Tony Restell, has produced some great content for candidates and recruiters alike, and following one of his sessions I started to look closer at Twitter, and found it great for striking up conversations and connections, that often then 'move the conversation across' to LinkedIn.

I recommend that you take a look at Twitter, as it's great for striking up discussions, and there are certainly more senior level colleagues, peers, and recruiters using Twitter than you might imagine.

6 – Jobs boards

Jobs boards are a necessary component in the job hunting jigsaw, but they're often somewhat underutilized by senior level executives. I fully understand the reticence to unleash your CV onto these jobs boards, as many candidates fear the inevitable *inappropriate* level job approaches, or just that feeling that you're not in control perhaps?

I have a recommended list of jobs boards which I am constantly updating, and it would be wrong to quote my favorites or any recommendations here, as it's a fast moving market.

What I would suggest is that you upload / register your CV to some selected jobs boards. You need a spread, as recruiters can gravitate toward certain ones, and these trends can change over time.

Once you have registered your information on a jobs board, it important to keep re-visiting it and updating your CV, so that it stays toward the "recent" end of updated CV's.

Why is this important as part of your overall job search strategy? CV's can be searched for by recruiters, and they may use a filter showing the *most recently updated* CV's, but also the results on any given search on a jobs board will naturally in most cases, bump the most recently "updated" to the top. Now of course, that update can be something minimal.

While having carefully crafted and selected keywords suitably included in your CV, there is one activity I would steer well clear of. This used to be called "white lining" or "white fonting", where keywords are listed at the bottom of a CV and saved as white text, in other words invisible.

This type of activity is needless to say highly frowned on by the recruitment industry, and guaranteed to get your CV binned if discovered, as software can now be used to detect this practice. Don't misunderstand me here; I don't imagine for one minute that you will try this yourself, but you should be aware of the activity. It could equally work against you if your CV got in front of some human eyes, who could not then see the keywords that brought the CV to their attention in the first place! Enough said.

'Kissing frogs' – part of the job hunt for sure, and it can be more prevalent with Jobs Boards as you may find yourself being approached for various (often not at all what you're looking for) opportunities by those who subscribe to that job boards data base. Just take the rough with the smooth.

So upload your CV and keep a weekly update schedule to remain 'current' *(making minor amendments to your CV will suffice)* on that particular job board.

7 – A Head Hunters View

Networking and interacting with recruiters

I interviewed top head hunter Phil Sharp, Managing Director of Executive Headhunters Ltd. My questions to Phil were based around some of the concerns my clients have. So here you have it from a Head Hunters perspective (My questions (Q) are in bold text):

Q: How can senior level candidates network appropriately?

I think the answer to this one really depends on whether the person is on the open job market or looking whilst still gainfully employed. For each case I think you need a different approach.

For a person openly looking, the first place I would start is by contacting any recruitment consultants they used to recruit staff for their previous business. If they don't operate at senior exec level they may have someone in their firm who does. As a previous "customer" it would be in that recruiters interests to prioritise your placement ahead of another candidate (on the assumption you will be a customer of the future)

I would also recommend working with one recruiter proactively to identify the top ten companies you want to work for (within your niche , don't pick Google, Facebook, Virgin etc., unless this is your niche. Recruiters are lazy so make it as easy as possible for them). Give this list to ONLY one recruitment business and give them a paragraph for each as to why you are a good fit for their business. A little preparation can have dramatic results.

Q: How to not be seen as desperate, yet follow up on opportunities appropriately?

Largely this would depend on what stage of the process you are at. It's perfectly reasonable to ask for timescales and next steps at each stage of the process and to follow up each time one of those timescales is met.

E.g. if contacted to send a CV, ask "When will I hear back from you?" If you don't hear, call them up.

After a head hunter / recruiter interview, "When will you have completed your shortlist?" Again, follow up if you don't hear.

If your details have been lodged with a head hunter more generally rather than against a specific brief, I'd say every few weeks is OK, or when a role appears on their site you feel matches your background.

Q: Perhaps a hot potato! I've been asked many times how to spot a real job from a fake?

Always down to level of detail and whether the head hunter is prepared to meet. If they are fishing for CVs the advert, or approach will be very generic and they won't commit to meeting you. Ask lots of questions, take charge and push for a face to face meeting with the recruiter. If they don't know the answers or are reluctant to meet, chances are it is indeed a CV fishing exercise.

Q: How to prepare for a recruiter interview?

Know your own CV inside out. Know WHY you are interested in the role if being interviewed for a specific role and MOST IMPORTANTLY why the end client should be chomping at the bit to meet you. What can you bring to the party that makes the potential new employer think "Now that's what we need!" – E.g. relationships with a key customer, knowledge of a technology, knowledge of a particular market etc., particularly if you can bring something to them that they don't have currently, but should have. E.g. experience launching in a new geographical area. Spell it out to the recruiter. "Your client doesn't sell in France. I work for a direct competitor that sells £10M pa in France and own all the relationships with the key distributors there..."

Q: What's your take Phil, on what really makes an impressive CV?

For me, both the exec summary and CV containing facts, figures, numbers, percentages. It's about immediate impact.

Any CV has to stand out. %£$€ symbols and numbers always leap off a CV when I read them. Too many words and no numbers make a CV dull. Virtually every role either exists to make or save a company money. Quantify everything in financial terms.

Q: I speak to so many people who are frustrated about not getting called back. Is this to do with the recruiter having already gathered a short list in most cases?

Depends on the circumstances. I'd say leave a detailed message if its voicemail with a "get-out" for the recruiter e.g. "Text me or email if I'm not of interest". Whilst not ideal, at least you will know you can discount it if looking at other things. On an average search, we speak to 100 to 200 people at first stage so it's not always possible to give detailed feedback at every stage. If you have been for any kind of interview though, either with the head hunter or client, you should expect verbal feedback. Anything else is plain ignorant.

Q: Is there anything else which would offer the reader a bit of an inside track?

Don't take things personally if a head hunter doesn't keep in regular contact. Chances are they have logged your details and background and will be in touch should they have something suitable. If they spent all their time returning every candidate call they wouldn't have time to service their clients. I know it's frustrating as a candidate. If you have been spoken to about a specific role, I would say its fine to contact them regularly until that opportunity progresses or is dead in the water.

I'd like to thank Phil for those insights; some hard hitting and really practical information there from a recruiter's perspective.

So to keep moving things forward, let's say you've got through the initial screening stages, and discover you have an interview. In the following chapter we'll look at some of the top strategies for making a good initial impression and describing your achievements in the best possible way.

8 – The Job Interview

"*No Fear? See the job interview as a meeting of equals. This mind set will help you relax and be yourself*".

What I will cover in this chapter reflects how we prepare clients for interview, together with some further insights from previous experiences and case studies. Of course, every person has different natural interview abilities, and areas that might need development.

Interview Skills for Senior Executives – what really makes a difference?

It's all pressure isn't it? Not only do we live and work in a fast paced world, but we also have to be ever adaptable in the world of work, ever-ready to adjust that CV, explore and list our skills and achievements, and so on.

There's so much information available these days about how to structure your CV and how to complete application forms (a rarer occurrence nowadays I appreciate) that I suspect this has directly impacted on the increasing levels of post-interview disappointment that I am always reading about. Why? Because we've become so much better at the "getting the interview" part, that candidates are often failing to then "walk the talk" during the interview (They simply don't have enough compelling 'war stories' to make what they look like on paper match how they present face to face). I'll cover this point in one of the following tips.

What can be done to improve your chances at the next job interview? I have a number of practical tips for your tool kit. Which ones you adopt will be a matter of personal choice. I strongly advocate all of them of course!

Job Interview & Mind Set Tips:

I've taken these selected job interview tips from many pre and post interview interactions with both clients and recruiters. I've found that no matter how much preparation you make, only a certain amount of it will "stick", so, these tips are based on some fundamentals.

- **Be tuned in, switched on in advance**

At least 15 minutes before you even enter the building, get "in the zone", relax, breathe (at least half a dozen slow inhale/exhales), tune in, and be absolutely *on your game.* Be fully in "interview mode". Don't leave it until you walk in the building to tune in. First impressions count as you know, and those first impressions can start at reception, particularly if the reception and other 'meet and greet' staff are involved in a 360 degree review process, which can happen more than you might expect. Don't let the first interaction you have with someone on entering the building (assuming a formal interview scenario here) be your first stumble.

- **"Walk the talk"**

You have ticked all of the boxes in the Job Description (JD), but do you have relevant and *engaging* 'war stories' (real examples) for the interviewer(s) that demonstrate that what you put down on paper lives and breathes for you. These anecdotes should be "locked and loaded" – ready to pull out of the bag as needed during the questioning process. That JD has been written for a reason, so read it, and read *between the lines* also. What are they really looking for in a candidate? Cover off the *desirables* as well as the *essentials* from the JD– assuming you can of course. When you're telling your *war stories*, be mindful of length of answer and format; in most competence based questions ('Tell me about a time when...' type of questions) following the STAR (Situation, Task, Action, Result) format is advisable. If you're answering a question and lose your way a bit, even remembering the R of STAR can get you back on track to focus in on the Result of the example you're quoting.

- **Rehearse**

This relates to the above point. I'd like you to dig a bit deeper, and work a bit harder at the whole *rehearsing the potential answers you might give* (to key questions which you will be able to anticipate, knowing the role's requirements). After thinking this through and writing them down, they should be rehearsed <u>aloud</u>, not in your head. Get used to the sound of your voice and it'll pay dividends in terms of confidence and credibility. I could write a book *just* about the benefits of rehearsing aloud; there is something that "locks in" the flow and wording much better by articulating aloud, than just reading the questions/answers on paper. Skip this one at your peril. There is no need to overdo the preparation. Start by writing out your answers for two or three questions, practice the answers, then do a couple more each day leading up to the interview. Even if the questions don't get asked in exactly the way that you anticipate, this level of preparation alone will set you apart from most other candidates.

- **Better company research**

A no brainer? Perhaps, but again, other candidates (your competitors for the role) are getting smarter at this. You can download an annual report, corporate plan, get tuned into the company's vision and objectives of course, but how about connecting with a few (non interview panel) employees via social networking, and by some gentle questioning/networking, finding out what the key issues and challenges are in the company? Is there any digging you can do via *Google news search* (also advisable doing this the day before the interview for any last minute company news) to find out *why* the role is available (i.e. what's the company's pain point, if any, that you can allude to during an interview), as well as being bang up to date re any news snippets relating the sector or competitors to throw into the conversation at the opportune moment?

- **Post interview note**

You will no doubt in the past have followed up an interview with an email note thanking the interviewers for their time, and briefly reiterating why you feel you're right for the role? If not, that's a must do. It's also an opportunity to reflect on the interview and to include new insights learned at the interview. But how about a *hand written, hand delivered thankyou card?* This can be written out beforehand, addressed to the interviewer(s), and left at reception as you leave (or if you're walked right to the exit, then pop back to reception just after!). I've known this gesture work many times on a number of levels. The main one is, whether you get the job or not, you will be remembered for such a personalized way of saying thank you, and I've known other opportunities emerge at a company following this strategy, which was remembered by the decision makers and a re-approach to the candidate in question resulted. I know this idea doesn't resonate for some, so as mentioned a short enthusiastic post-interview *thank you* email, reiterating the key points that came out of the interview and how you match them, is the bare minimum, as well as the debrief with your head hunter or recruiter.

- **It's a 'business meeting'**

This is all about state of mind. If you truly view the interview as a *business meeting*, it will change the way you approach things slightly – you'll feel a bit more like you're sharing the 'driving seat', and I've known many cases where the candidate has been successful by adopting this mind-set (and having conducted many real, and mock interviews I can tell you it comes across as impressive). Certain interview contexts don't allow for as much interaction, such as some public sector processes where interview answers are being scored, leading to little opportunity for additional interaction between the questions. In a more corporate business environment however the more that you can get into a meaningful dialogue, as well as ensuring you're ticking the boxes as you progress, will stand you in good stead.

- **How to make a fast positive impact**

We've all heard of the 10-20 second decision, where the interviewer subconsciously makes a decision about you within a seemingly short space of time. How can you make an impact in those vital first few seconds?

Another key question in an increasingly competitive c-level jobs market is how do you show that you add value and importantly (when up against other similarly qualified candidates) how do you *differentiate* yourself? Here's how I would suggest you approach these:

- **Personal Chemistry**

I'll cover this first; regardless of how well you are able to put across your skills, you need to work on *creating rapport* – in a big way. So take a look at the interviewers LinkedIn profile. Are there are hobbies that you have in common? Did you go to the same University? Perhaps you did an MBA at the same place? What about the company's annual report or in-house (if you can access it) newsletter? Are there any snippets of useful info that you can throw into the conversation early on? Demonstrating insights have a great impact and are memorable.

Don't get me wrong here, you either hit it off or you don't with any given individual in life. We all know that, but there's no harm in seeking some personal common ground if you can. Underestimate the power of being personable at your peril!

- **Step into their shoes**

If you're being interviewed by a Chairman, CEO, Panel, NED, whoever it might be, it's vital to put yourself in their shoes.
- What makes them tick?
- What motivates them?
- Why do they need someone in the role now?
- What's the broader picture?

Having this mind set will help to ensure that you're not just reeling off skills/abilities where you think it's appropriate, but that you're focussing on seeing *what matters to them.*

- **Repetition builds Reputation**

A somewhat "corny" sounding phrase harking back to my advertising sales days many moons ago, but I think it holds true in an interview situation; *caveat* when used with subtlety. The phrase *repetition builds reputation* was originally designed to encourage repeat advertising, but in an interview context you sometimes have to make a point two or three times before it sticks in the interviewers memory, so throughout the interview I suggest focussing on your personal added value, and keep coming back to your key points of differentiation (or value proposition) – not overly so (you be the judge), but two or three mentions of a key point would be fine.

- **The 2 or 3%**

This is a phrase that perhaps I coined (not sure about that one), but in any case it relates to the *small difference* there is likely to be between you and the other candidates for the c-level role you're going for. So be memorable (in a good way) and ensure that you state your case thoroughly in the interview. For me, a lot of it comes down to personal chemistry as I've mentioned, which is difficult to "teach", but it's certainly something that I focus on. The remainder falls into the "what additional digging can I do that other candidates may not have done?" category.

9 – 'Soft' Skills & their importance

"Emotional Intelligence (EQ) is a major factor in career success, and career progression in general".

When my company starts working with a new client, there are some fundamental areas we discuss, but one factor that we always mention is that some areas that need addressing or working on are often *veiled* at any early conversation stage. They can include factors around confidence, networking ability and on some occasions *blind spots.*

The following story demonstrates the benefit of being aware and highly personable during the job interview process

How being personable can make a big difference

- Prepared for that upcoming job interview?

- Clothes pressed, shoes shined, answers rehearsed?

While I am a massive advocate of properly rehearsing the answers to potential interview questions (I make no apology for "soap-boxing" here. There really is no excuse these days not to have prepared in this way), I would urge you to take into account another point, one which can make a major difference. It's a classic example of small things can make big difference. Don't underestimate the power of rapport building and *simply being personable…*

A good friend (and client by default) of mine recently attended a typically gruelling high level industry interview. You know, one of those processes that take an entire day (but perhaps feels longer) or more. This was for a post with an excellent salary and benefits to die for, including an idyllic working location. The interview process involved presentations, panel interviews, tour of the company premises (by the way, however well you may know the building where your interview is to be conducted, *never* refuse the invitation to have a guided tour. The information you will pick up during this more informal stage of the interview process can be invaluable during the interview itself, and is a prime opportunity to find out what issues staff are facing, things that need addressing etc.), and to top it all off my friend was then asked to give an impromptu speech to the assembled staff – scary stuff!

I also loved the way he had spent some time touring the coastal setting for this interview, and took some photos which he used in the backdrop to his PowerPoint presentation later that day; something which the panel liked, and just shows that *little extra touch*. This can apply to any level of job, and demonstrates the human side of the interview process very well. We are all human, and those little touches are often appreciated, even though we may not realise it at the time.

He was appointed into the post a few days later, and is now thriving in a role which is enjoyable as well as challenging.

We met up a few days later for a coffee, and after listening to his story he asked me, "What do you think was a major factor in my being appointed?" After I had volunteered *two* reasons (ok, so I know him well, which helped that time!) which were both correct, it led to me wanting to share this with all of you. Reason one was the PowerPoint pictures I mentioned above, but the biggest reason? When he arrived at the building for the interview he spent a good ten minutes chatting with the reception staff asking questions such as, "How long have you been working here?" "What's it like here?" What he didn't know at the time that the company included all staff that candidates were exposed to as part of a 360 degree feedback process. He had, however, noticed other candidates arriving and after signing in, swanning past reception with a cursory nod. Little did they know the error they had already made.

I hope that little story gives you a clue as to how vital being personable and having due regard for all things 'emotional intelligence' are?

What do you do if your motivation and mind-set taking a bit of a hammering during a   job search?

I would like to share a story with you around motivation and resilience:

After a client meeting recently where we had been discussing the fact that my client knew they could probably be doing more in terms of networking, I started to reflect on the whole subject of motivation and internal "resilience", and I was reminded of a time when my resilience almost failed me...

I wanted to raise some money for a charity I supported by doing an 80 mile off road ride on my trusty mountain bike. This involved 8 trips back and forth along a 10 mile route that I was familiar with, but had only ever done 20 miles at one time.

The worst leg of the trip was during the 7th 10 mile stretch. I had really physically seized up by that point, and I got to a bend in the track where I saw a patch of grass. I skidded to a halt (not that I was going that fast by then!), lay the bike down, got down on the ground and just lay there with my eyes closed, feeling nauseous... I was done, finished, and only a leg and a bit away from achieving my goal.

To cap it all I couldn't let my family (who were meeting me at the next stage) know that this had happened, as there was no mobile phone signal. After a few minutes of simply breathing, centring myself and gathering my thoughts, I said to myself, "Get up, keep going. If you don't do this no one else is going to". So I got up, pushed off, and eventually made it to the penultimate checkpoint. The last leg of the challenge was pure adrenaline, and spookily easy considering what had just happened on the previous leg.

It can be like this when job hunting; the early enthusiasm, motivation and systematized approach can start to wane a few months in, particularly when achieving your next senior role can take a while. You might start to take your 'foot off the gas' in terms of the numbers of meetings you're arranging and the general networking and job application levels can dip. I understand how that can feel. To check where you are in terms of motivation ask yourself the following questions:

Am I consistently engaging with people in LinkedIn groups, and other relevant platforms to leverage the hidden jobs market?

Am I keeping track of meetings I've had, and follow ups due?

Am I presenting the right personal brand to the market?

Do I have a weekly LinkedIn strategy for engagement and connections?

Am I keeping in touch with head hunters and recruiters?

Am I as motivated as I was 3, 6, 9 months ago?

If you have a bad day during the job search then take that day off for sure, but I wouldn't suggest that let this become a second and third day

10 - FAQ's

The following are my take on questions that we are often asked during the hundreds of discussions that we have with senior level executives.

How do I handle job search frustration?

During any job hunt whether you are employed and trying to get out of your existing role, or perhaps you've not been working for sometimes, it does get frustrating, and the most important thing to focus on if called for a recruiter or employer interview is to *try not to transmit that frustration* through to the interviewer(s). So, coming from a position of strength and confidence is much, much better. I advise you to take some time off from that daily job hunt grind. Get out of your office/study, go for a walk, do whatever you do: but, just make sure you actually get some time to give yourself some *brain space*. Also, exercising [even just walking] is really, really good for that (I often find that simply walking allows the creative side to work, and new ideas often come when we're not trying quite so hard). If you have a really bad day, just give yourself a day off, but I would urge no more than one day. So you should be 'back on the horse' the following day and keep doing that networking, connecting, and keep pushing forward. It's the only way you're going to win that role. Resilience is critical.

What are your top job interview tips?

I've covered some of these already, but here are some more: The four Rs: research, rehearse, rapport, and results. I might have invented this four R's process but if not, I apologize. *Research*: high-level research - not just usual stuff. Find out *why* the role you're applying for exists in the first place, or what is happening with the competition in that sector. *Rehearse*: As in, rehearse your answers to anticipated questions and rehearse them *aloud*. It is good to get used to the sound of your own voice in that context. *Rapport*: When you are at an interview, be mindful of the need to build rapport. They need to like you, they need to know they can work with you, and they need to know whether you can fit in. And *Result*: Remember about the STAR format: situation, task, action, which is a good format to use within an interview answer context as well. So there you go! The 4Rs. Adopt these simple rules and it can really give you an edge in your next job interview.

Why don't recruiters call me back?

Why don't recruiters contact you after you have been submitted for a role? You wait for your phone to ring, it doesn't ring. You send an email, nothing. You call and leave a voicemail, and you don't hear anything back. I do feel your pain, I truly do. It might help you in some ways to understand that a recruiter is motivated by gathering a shortlist for a specific assignment that they might be working on. Their whole business model is focused on getting someone appointed into a role, because that's when they get paid. Having said that, I think there should be better communication in a lot of cases, e.g. just to actually come back to you to say why you were not taken any further in that particular process. They have to service their clients too, so keep this in mind as well, but I'd say this is the number one complaint among candidates that I speak with; particularly as senior level executives could be the recruiter's clients one day.

What am I supposed to do with social media?

Social media - in terms of personal branding requires a bit of thought, planning and engagement. As a senior level candidate, you primarily would be using LinkedIn I would hazard a guess. But also, what is the value of Twitter, Google+? With Twitter you have that immediacy of engagement (no connect request process), plus *there are more recruiters and senior level executive peers on Twitter than you might imagine.* Google+ is more about where you rank on Google search, so having a presence there is more likely to see any Google search for keywords that could 'hit' your profile, seeing your results further toward page one of Google, or even on page one itself. My general advice is to be consistent and business-like across all of these platforms. Remember you're going to be researched by a recruiter by looking you up on social media. You need to make sure that your brand and value proposition across all types of social media represent you in a way you would be proud of and would not embarrass you in any way. So, be consistent, and have a clear message about who you are and what you have to offer, as that can drive your value upwards and 'raise your stock' so to speak.

Am I too old for a new role or a career change?

I get a number of top executives who have talked to me about their concern about being perceived as being too old for a role. It is the one area I would advise having 'blinkers on'. You cannot change the way the other people think about you. But you can change the way you think. So, re-concentrate on your value preposition that you would bring to that particular role and do not let the "Gremlins" get in the way. Age really is just a number, and anyone who seems to think differently, drop them, and move on to more positive people. I've mentioned resilience before, but this is another area where it's important.

What do I have to do to get promoted?

This subject might interest those of who are thinking about networking for promotion. I speak to some people who are just below board level and looking to make that next step up. There are many, many ways I would suggest you could do this depending on your individual circumstances and preferences but I will say a couple of them would be: to try to find any mentor or someone who can guide you through that process within your own organization or even externally: someone who is working at that level. You can just absorb that learning from meeting them on a weekly or even on a monthly basis, something regular though that's in your diary is what I'd suggest. Secondly, read about the leaders that you admire. What they do and how do they act / present themselves. But it should be the people you actually admire. So, you can follow somebody's posts on LinkedIn for example. Those are just a couple of quick tips on networking for promotion.

Do I *really* need an elevator pitch?

Yes you do. I talk to clients at length about structure and how you should position yourself to the best effect, and an elevator pitch is simply a smart arrow to have in your career planning quiver. For an elevator pitch (based on talking with a recruiter primarily), we're talking about 30 - 60 seconds in length: so be very clear about your value; think beginning, middle, end, with ideally a nice £$%€ piece of info in the middle to show tangible achievement *Rehearsing* (yes, I'm mentioning rehearsing aloud again) is key, so that when you're called on to launch into your pitch, that you can do so naturally, rather than like you've never said those words before in your life!

What do I do after connecting with people on social media?

My key advice here is to follow up those connections once you have made an initial connection. You'd be surprised how many people don't. I was reminded of this recently by a friend of mine who said, *"Actually, I have got lots of connections, even though I do not have many conversations."* So, the lesson here is really to review who you are connected with and rather than keep ploughing through the emailing process. See if you can get the telephone number, pick the telephone and have a chat, and see if you can arrange up *an actual appointed call with them* on an introductory basis. So try picking up the phone just for a change rather than relying on email totally. This can be a breath of fresh air in your job search.

How do I get the most out of LinkedIn groups?

If you are going to join groups, I suggest you join some across three different categories. And I am talking to, of course, senior level executives here. Industry sector - the seniority level of discipline of the role - say, CFO, MD, etc., types of groups. And then, thirdly, some head hunter/recruiter type groups as well. Do your due diligence with each of these as described earlier in the book. Going to the group settings and find out if they're primarily EU, UK, US, focused. Is that you are looking for? There's little point joining a group if it's going to be of little value. Have a look at the membership, make sure it's an appropriate seniority level as well, and then, start gradually to *like* some things. Start to engage. You've got to raise your visibility, so the whole point of these groups and your activity in them is to drive traffic back to your profile with a view to help open a new door, or unlock the hidden jobs market.

However, some candidates just do not feel comfortable doing any of this kind of networking. At the very least, use the members tab in LinkedIn groups to identify (via the search box) head hunters, recruiters, or senior peers of interest, which you can then message (rather than sending a stilted connect request) by virtue of the fact that you're both in the same group. This will give you the chance to outline your value and aims, and *invite them onto a call* (a *call to action* is important with any networking).

11 – Time for a Career Change?

"We all have varying life goals, dreams, and aspirations".

Have you ever considered a complete career change?

This chapter is aimed at those of you who are looking at an entire change in direction, and explores some of the factors to consider.

First it's vital to explore "You" – The importance of stepping back and taking a breath when changing career.

If, like me, you've ever considered a career change (This is just as relevant if you're looking to develop your current career or take *step change*), then I suggest that you stop, take a breath, and formulate a plan which includes as many factors about "you" as possible (Likes, Strengths, Values, Ideal working environment, to name a few).

Of course skills, qualifications and abilities are vital, but when I discuss this with clients, it often transpires that they have not stopped to consider what they "really want". So slow down. Point one.

It's natural to some extent to want to just move on quickly, but this research and reflection time will be time very well spent.

I suggest that you jot down some notes at this stage, because what I'm offering here is a structure that you can work through in order to reveal aspects of yourself that you weren't aware of, or perhaps had forgotten about.

Ok, so to begin with take a deep breath, we need to get a complete 'picture' of you; likes, dislikes, strengths, values, goals... It can take time, because the natural urge is to just job hunt. How do you get this picture in place? *I suggest you get started by writing a short biography* (200-300 words), and to look at your highs and lows over the past, so that you can create as full a picture as possible of "you".

What have you achieved in your career that you're proud of?
What did you really enjoy?
What problems or challenges have you encountered over the years, and how did you overcome these?

Following these suggestions will give you as full a picture as possible of "you". Some tips:

- When writing your biography, look for clues to your *values*, and write them down. *Values* are a vital element to finding the right career.
- Be positive. Always. Write down ten things that you *like* about yourself. This can be a challenge, but will help your mind-set. Don't succumb to the temptation of skipping this piece!
- Think about whether you're naturally a risk taker career-wise. If so what happened when you took risks? What happened when you didn't?
- In tandem with the above, start to generate career ideas/factors that appeal to you. Keep this "ideas file" as a list, spreadsheet, collage, whatever works for you.

Keep updating this list with new ideas as you go about your day. Be in a 'constant mode of enquiry', as I call it.

Taking time to think about "you" fully can also be a fun stage where "light bulbs" going on regularly, as realizations about past errors in career strategy are realised, and a plan to move forward is gradually laid down. This is a thorough process, and I again urge you to take the time to explore all of your values, strengths, likes, and desires before rushing into job search.

After the *exploration* phase I suggest that you enter what I call the *blue sky* phase. This is an exciting and challenging stage where you get to think outside of the box, be creative, and really go for it!

What careers have you ever dreamt of doing? What jobs did you dream about when you were 6 years old? 11 years old? 16 years old? – No, don't "*edit*" yourself". This is brainstorming, so anything goes. Pragmatism will come later in the process.

By using the exercises you've done previously, and your own *intuition*, try to get down to three job/career possibilities (aside from the fact that you may already have clear ideas about your chosen path). All three possibilities should meet your values, skills and abilities, and be something you *feel truly passionate* about. All three ideas should also stack up against all of the aspects of Life and

Work, which you will have been recording throughout. After we have those three ideas (through the coaching process) we then get to one idea. It's this idea which you will take forward and formulate a plan of action to get you there. How do you get from three options to one? I suggest you ask yourself some searching questions:

- Referring back to the previous exercises, really drill deep down into each choice. Which makes you feel really enthusiastic?
- Ask yourself the potential pro's and con's for each choice
- Paint a "Word Picture" for each choice; visualize yourself doing the role in the future – write it down. How does it feel? What are you doing? Why do you love it so much? Could it be better?
- What results would you like to create for each possibility?
- Your final choice should be the one that's most "alive" for you. Of course, this process is something we would normally discuss with you during coaching.

Finally, I suggest that you create a practical, detailed action plan. Decide who you need to contact (or other action required), by when, and for what reason. This detailed list of action points is vital to carry the whole process forward. I cannot emphasise enough that this is all for nought without 'execution' and 'review'.

You've heard of *smart* action planning, and most probably heard of smarter action planning too, but how often is *execution and review* missing from this equation?

This chapter outlines just some of the processes we take our career coaching clients through, and forms part of our career change programme, which has helped hundreds of people to find their ideal career. It can only be an overview of the process I'd suggest, but I'd like to emphasise that exploration is the key piece of work here, and is absolutely crucial.

So the take away for this chapter is that I hope you take the time to step back, take that breath (and have completed some of the exercises mention?), before embarking on a career path that just might not suit you.

12 - Your next steps and *action*

"It's all for naught without action"

This could be the most important chapter in this book, and definitely the shortest.

I suggest you revisit the chapters you most enjoyed and start to write an *action plan* (using the Notes pages at the end of this book if they help). A daily plan of action is what I would suggest a concerted effort across social media engagement & networking, CV updating, and interview skills practice. Your job hunt could take many months (not uncommon at senior level) so you need a plan, but one which builds in time to get away from the computer/tablet/phone etc, retains your sanity and energy levels, and keeps you fresh for those interviews!

You don't need to spend hours and hours every day at the job search activity. In fact I'd suggest allocating a set amount of time and sticking to it as far as possible. I often use the timer function on my smart phone, as it keeps me focused on any given task.

I also advocate good old *post it notes*. Just a couple: one with your key goal during your job search campaign, and another with your three main skills that you can bring to the table (in exactly the same way as the two elevator pitches I described earlier). Keep them above your computer desk, or wherever you work at home, so that you see them whenever you are there.

I'm 100% sure you'll know about SMART action planning, so I'm not even going to define the acronym, but I found an extended version of this more useful in ensuring that any goals we set are regularly reviewed and acted upon. Think *SMART-ER* action planning: adding *Execution* and *Review*. Without those two additional elements, the cycle of the job search task can stumble.

After establishing your career strategy, keep pushing forward, hold yourself accountable (or get someone to hold you accountable), maintain high levels of resilience, and I wish you every success in landing your next senior executive role.

An Invitation

If you'd like to find out more about how we work with senior executives and help them to secure their next role, I'd invite you to have a confidential call to discuss your situation and career goals.

For 30 minutes, we will explore the challenges that you're facing or questions you may have, in an open and honest "same side of the table" style of meeting (via Skype most often).

You will receive some advice and suggestions as to the best way forward, based on what you have told us about your individual situation.

The process will improve the odds of your landing your next role sooner – and you'll be a better informed candidate.

You will not be put under any pressure at any stage of the discussion. What you will receive however are actionable concrete tips to help move you forward.

Then if we agree that we can be of further assistance in your situation, we'll explain how we can help.

The only criteria are that you're a senior level executive seeking your next role, and that you're open to the idea of working with a coach.

To arrange a call visit:
www.executivecconnexions.co.uk/book-a-call
or email me direct at
contact@executiveconnexions.co.uk

About the Author

Steve Nicholls

I am currently Managing Director of Executive Connexions Ltd., an executive career coaching company with a worldwide clientele, which I invite you to visit at www.executiveconnexions.co.uk (or .com, or .eu, or .uk as you prefer).

My key role is to actively support senior executives to find their next role... the next step in their career if you will. It's something I thoroughly enjoy, and I get a real buzz every time a client has a 'light bulb moment' whether through having had a storming job interview, or that moment when they 'get' a certain point we've been discussing during coaching sessions.

My company's client base is an international one, made up of senior level executives working across a range of sectors, and I have learned much that I've tried to share in this book, having found that despite cultural and geographical nuances; there are many areas of common concern and focus when approaching the subject of searching for a new role.

Our aim is to ensure that others seeking their next role achieve this aim with the minimum of fuss and complexity, and we hope you will find this pragmatic approach is reflected in the pages of this book.

Life and Career

Growing up, I was always the quiet one in a group, a natural introvert, with a high level of emotional intelligence and an ability to read between the lines of any given conversation. Maybe part of that was due to being an only child, but I always found listening more interesting than talking; learning about people, offering advice when sought, and these traits have followed me into adult life and my own career, which has led me from character forming careers in the Metropolitan Police in London at 18, followed by experience in advertising sales & publishing, business consultancy, the charity sector, through to retraining for two years as a careers adviser in the mid 90's.

My career has taken me from the countryside in Cornwall to the bright lights of London, and I now live and work between both locations, spending most of my time in Cornwall.

By visiting our website you will gain access to a plethora of useful articles, podcasts, and reports which I hope will supplement the information in this book.

Let's get social

If you use any or all of the social media platforms below, then we'd be happy to connect.

LinkedIn (my page):
uk.linkedin.com/in/stevenichollsexecconnexions/

LinkedIn (company page):
https://www.linkedin.com/company/executive-connexions-ltd-

Twitter (my page):
https://twitter.com/SNCareerCoach/

Twitter (company page):
https://twitter.com/ExecConnexions/

Google+ (my page):
https://plus.google.com/+SteveNichollsCareerCoach/posts

Google+ (company page):
https://plus.google.com/b/114064198905747770180/

Facebook Company Page:
https://www.facebook.com/SNCareerCoach

Notes

Three interview questions that the interviewer is *really* asking themselves? *Do I like them? Can they do the job? Will they fit in here?*

Notes

Get as much £$%€ info onto your CV/Resume as you can. Recruiters and employers eyes are drawn to this information.

Notes

Elevator Pitch Primer:

1. Intro to you, discipline, sector

2. Value you have brought previously (one or two "knock out punches" (i.e. £$%€ info/achievements are ideal here)

3. Aspirational piece – what are you now looking for?

Notes

Remember to use the 'STAR' format in relation to the CV/Resume *and* at interview.

Notes

*Stop connecting & **start calling.*** Not literally of course (re stopping connecting), but sometimes picking up the phone and following up new contacts by phone is a pleasant change and can yield surprising results.

Notes

Before the interview practice aloud – *yes aloud* – the answers you might give to anticipated questions. This practice will pay off regardless of the exact questions asked, as you will feel better prepared.

Visit us at

Made in the USA
Charleston, SC
29 January 2015